THE NATIONAL AUDUBON SOCIETY COLLECTION
NATURE SERIES

NORTH AMERICAN
MAMMALS

THE NATIONAL AUDUBON SOCIETY COLLECTION
NATURE SERIES

NORTH AMERICAN
MAMMALS

Text by Barbara Burn

Foreword by James Doherty, General Curator,
The New York Zoological Society

Bonanza Books • New York

All of the photographs in this book are from Photo Researchers/National Audubon Society Collection. The name of the individual photographer follows each caption.

Photographers' credits for uncaptioned photographs in the front and back matter of this book are (in order of appearance): Joe Rychetnik, Jan Lindblad, Stephen J. Krasemann, Pat and Tom Leeson, Leonard Lee Rue III, Sturgis McKeever, Leonard Lee Rue III, Stephen J. Krasemann, Russ Kinne, Tom McHugh, Cosmos Blank, and G. C. Kelley.

I wish to express my deep appreciation to Christian Dolensek for his help in doing research for this book and to Jim Doherty of the New York Zoological Society (The Bronx Zoo) for both his willingness to read the text and his helpful suggestions. Any errors that may appear here, however, are entirely my own.—Barbara Burn

---

The National Audubon Society Collection Nature Series
Staff for this book
General Editor: Robin Corey
Photo Researcher: Tim Quinson
Production Editor: Jean T. Davis
Designer: June Marie Bennett
Production Manager: Laura Torrecilla
Production Supervisor: Cindy Lake

This 1984 edition is published by Bonanza Books, distributed by Crown Publishers, Inc., One Park Avenue, New York, New York 10016

Manufactured in Italy

Library of Congress Cataloging in Publication Data
Burn, Barbara. North American mammals.
(The National Audubon Society collection nature series)
Includes index. 1. Mammals—North America.
I. National Audubon Society. II. Title. III. Series.
QL715.B79 1984 599.097 83-24016

ISBN: 0-517-447436

h g f e d c b a

CONTENTS

CONTENTS

THE NATIONAL AUDUBON SOCIETY COLLECTION
NATURE SERIES

NORTH AMERICAN
MAMMALS

FOREWORD

Here is a book that deals with the mammals of the world—not all the mammals of the world but species of mammals native to North America that represent most of the orders of mammals surviving today. In choosing the mammals for this book importance has been placed not only on the well-known or more characteristic species but also on those that are in some way unique or distinct.

What is a mammal? It is any vertebrate, an animal with a backbone, that nurses its offspring on the milk from the mother's mammary glands. Mammals—and *only* mammals—have hair, although some of the large aquatic species may have a few bristles, and even these may be lost in some adults.

Mammals are so successful and numerous that they can be found on every continent and in every ocean in the world, living in many diverse habitats. Blue whales and bats, echidnas and elephants, are but a few members of a class filled with wonderful diversity.

This book is not intended as a field guide for those of you fortunate enough to live close to wild animals or able to visit areas where wild animals live. Few of us will ever be fortunate enough to see many of the mammals discussed on these pages unless we see them in a zoo or aquarium, although some will never be seen in captivity. Read this book and consider it an introduction to the wonderful world of mammals. Although it focuses on North American species, you will learn much about all mammals and it will have you thinking differently about them—even your pet dog or cat.

JAMES DOHERTY
General Curator
1984 The New York Zoological Society

9

INTRODUCTION

The marten, a predatory animal, is active throughout the winter months.
(Russ Kinne)

Welcome to the world of North American mammals. It is a fascinating world—full of familiar faces but with plenty of surprises as well. Although there are fewer mammals on this continent than there are birds and insects, we humans feel a greater affinity for them than for other animals, probably because we are mammals ourselves. We may admire the grandeur of the bald eagle and the beauty of the monarch butterfly, but we sense a much warmer kinship with the fawn of a white-tailed deer or the impressive grizzly bear with its two-footed stance. All mammals have a similar body structure, and we humans produce and raise our off-spring much as the tiny harvest mouse and the huge musk-ox do, different as we and these animals are in so many other ways. Some mammals, such as wolves and bats, are feared by humans; others, such as rats and weasels, are despised; and some are even killed deliberately, whether for food, for fur, or simply for sport. Nevertheless, we feel a special sympathy for most of our fellow mammals, both wild and domestic.

The North American continent is exceptionally rich in native wild mammals. Of the nineteen orders (or major groups) of mammals in the world, North America is home to more than half—and what a wide variety there is. We have no tigers here, but we do have mountain lions and bobcats; we don't have the elephant or rhinoceros, but we have the pronghorn, one of the world's fastest-running animals. Our mammals range in size from the tiny pygmy shrew, which weighs only one-eighth of an ounce, to the blue whale, which can weigh up to 150 tons. Some mammals spend their lives almost entirely underground or underwater, while others have adapted to life in trees and

Caribou, which are members of the deer family, are also known in Europe as reindeer. They migrate over long distances in the spring. (Stephen J. Krasemann)

hardly ever touch the ground.

It is not easy to study mammals in the wild, for they are almost always shy and secretive and thus difficult to find. Domestic animals, because they have lived for years with humans, have lost their fear of us, but most wild mammals, even the largest ones, tend to flee from us, leaving only a footprint or some other subtle sign that they have been in the vicinity. Squirrels and rabbits may show themselves for the sake of a peanut or a carrot, but on a typical stroll through the woods, we are far more likely to see birds, frogs, and turtles than we are to spot a deer or a badger. One reason for this is that many mammals are nocturnal, coming out of their sleeping places to look for food only at dusk or during the night, partly because that is when food is readily available and partly because the darkness protects them from enemies. A number of mammals are protected in the daytime by camouflage—coloring or markings that blend in with their surroundings—while others have extremely well-developed senses of hearing and sight that en-

able them to hear or see danger in time to run, hide, or, if necessary, fight tooth and nail in self-defense. These defense mechanisms have all developed as a result of what scientists call adaptation, and this is perhaps the most intriguing part of the study of animals, since it has led to many interesting variations in behavior and appearance in all forms of animal life.

Millions of years ago, in the age of dinosaurs, mammals did not exist as they do today. The great reptiles of the Mesozoic period were the dominant species. The reptiles from which mammals eventually evolved—our ancestors—were a special group called synapsids. They were tiny shrewlike creatures that spent most of their time keeping out of harm's way. As the dinosaurs died out, the synapsids became more and more successful, growing in size and number until they were themselves dominant. The evolutionary process through which they became mammals and took the different shapes they have today is a very complex one, but in essence it involved adaptation. Some mammals have re-

These two animals, a prairie dog (left) and a beaver (facing page), are both in the rodent group but are adapted to very different life-styles.
(Tom McHugh)

tained the small size of the synapsids, as well as the ability to detect danger and escape it. These small mammals are very quick and alert, and they need to eat relatively large quantities of food—usually seeds or insects—to maintain themselves. They also give birth to many offspring, making it more likely that at least a few survive to adulthood. Other mammals became much larger and had to adapt to different sources of food—grasses, fruits, and even other animals. The grazing animals naturally moved to vast, grass-covered plains where many banded together in herds to protect themselves against predators; these animals developed hooves to help them run quickly over the terrain, and some of them have even become especially adept at coping with rocky areas as well as the prairies. Meat-eating mammals gradually acquired the ability to track and hunt for their food, developing aggressive instincts along with effective teeth and claws to serve as weaponry. These mammals, because they are so fiercely competitive with one another for food, tend to be relatively solitary (although a few—the wolf and the coyote, for instance—have learned to work together in pairs or packs), and their numbers have remained limited, since they produce few offspring and require large territories to support themselves. A few mammals have been so adaptable that they can survive on both vegetation and meat—whichever is most plentiful—and these omnivores, like humans, are among the most successful mammals of all.

Food is not the only reason for animals to adapt, however. Habitat—the area in which an animal lives—has had a great deal to do with the fact that mammals are among the most varied of all types of animals. It is amazing to think that our own mammal relatives have been able to survive in such inhospitable environments as deserts, the Arctic tundra, even the sea itself, and all without air conditioning, central heating, or deep-sea diving equipment. This ability to withstand extremes in temperature is one of the secrets of mammalian success, for each of us has a built-in thermostat that enables us to adjust our body heat to our surroundings. In the cold, our metabolism and heart rate speed up to produce heat, and in warm weather we can sweat or pant to lose heat and become cool. Most mammals have fur rather than scales or feathers, and this also acts as a temperature control, although it also works to protect the skin and, in some species, such as the porcupine, acts as a

The prairie dog digs a burrow for its home in the open grasslands of the Midwest, while the beaver has developed the ability to construct hugh, elaborate dams in his watery habitat to support the lodge in which he sleeps and raises his family. (Harry Engels)

defense mechanism as well. Animals that do not have a great deal of fur—humans, whales, and some desert animals—usually have an insulating layer of fat under the skin.

It is interesting to note that many animals that are very different have developed similar physical attributes because of their environment. Aquatic animals as different as the muskrat and the sea otter have webbed feet to help them swim, while several arctic animals—the arctic fox, the snowshoe hare, the lynx, and the polar bear—have fur on their feet that helps them travel comfortably on snow and ice. The limbs of some mammals, such as the flying squirrels and the many species of bats, have become so specialized that they can even glide or fly through the air.

Behavior, of course, has developed alongside these physical changes, as each animal species has learned over the eons to stay alive and to raise its young in different types of habitats. One fine example of the power of adaptation can be seen in a comparison of the prairie dog and the beaver, two closely related members of the rodent order. The flat, open spaces of the Midwest offer very little protection against the cold winter weather, so the prairie dog working along with thousands of its kind has learned to build extremely complex underground burrows often covering areas of a hundred acres or more. The beaver, on the other hand, living alongside rivers and ponds in forested areas, has developed a much different form of construction—elaborate dams made from logs and mud to contain its living quarters. While the prairie dog uses a high-pitched yelp to warn its neighbors of danger, the beaver prefers to slap its tail on the water as an alarm, a much more effective signal in its particular habitat.

Each of these remarkable adaptations was not made in isolation, of course, but in coordination with a number of other animals, since many mammals share the same habitat, along with birds, reptiles, and insects. It is the interrelationship among these animals and the environment of plants, rocks, earth, and water around them that we call ecology, which is simply a scientific term for the intricate web of nature in which each element plays an important part. If one animal were to disappear, the balance would be disrupted, however slightly, until adaptations took place to restore the balance. That animal's niche or place in the ecological system might be left empty, or it might be filled by a new animal, either introduced from another area or moving in from another niche in the same habitat.

One particularly interesting example of this change is the wild mustang. Millions of years ago, there were horses on the North American continent, but they disappeared over time, having been hunted out, chased away, or killed off by disease or accident. When the European settlers came here, they brought domestic horses with them; a few got loose and were able to survive on their own in certain areas in the West—probably the same areas where horses had once roamed wild. Although the present-day mustangs are not true wild horses but descendants of the domestic species, they have adapted to life in the wild as "feral" animals without disturbing the natural ecology very much, since

they fitted into the niche once occupied by their long-ago relatives. There are a number of similar cases where introduced foreign animals—wild or domestic—have become feral, and these species will be included in this book as well, along with some of the domestic mammals that share the continent with the wild ones. It is not difficult to see that the wolf and the dog are cousins under the skin, or that cattle and bison are from the same bovine family. But the differences are perhaps more interesting than the similarities, for that is where the versatile hand of nature can be clearly seen.

The introduced species that has had the greatest impact on North American ecology—not all of it for the good—is man himself, and in this book we will see many examples of our own interference with the balance of nature. Some of the changes we have made were deliberate, eliminating animals because they were either valuable or harmful to us, but the greatest change has been an inadvertent one, as our living space has intruded on what was once the exclusive domain of our fellow creatures, making it difficult or impossible for them to live normal lives. Fortunately, many of us feel a sense of responsibility for these animals and have made an effort not only to help conserve them but also to learn more about the ways in which they live. Because we live in developed areas where there are more people than animals and more buildings than trees, we must rely on the knowledge of experts in the field to "see" wild animals as easily as we can see their domestic counterparts. The photographs in this book were made by specialists who have spent years studying the behavior of their subjects in order to know where and when they can be found. Thanks to them and to the research done by scientists who have observed animals in the wild, we can begin to appreciate the immense richness of our own land and the creatures that share it with us.

Although the mustang is a familiar sight in the "wild" West, it is not actually native to North America but was introduced by Europeans, whose horses escaped and learned to fend for themselves. (Gianni Tortoli)

PRIMITIVE MAMMALS

Contrary to its tanklike appearance, the nine-banded armadillo of the southern United States is actually a mild-mannered creature that spends most of its time foraging for food. (Dave Norris; see page 20.)

We often use the word *primitive* to mean crude or uncivilized, but in the animal kingdom, *primitive* actually implies success, since it refers to groups of early animals that have survived for millions of years with little need to change or adapt to new conditions.

THE MARSUPIALS

One of the most primitive types of mammal is the marsupial—named for the marsupium, or pouch, in which it raises its young. Marsupials do not develop a placenta as more evolved mammals do to nurture unborn offspring

In spite of its name, the Virginia opossum is actually found in many parts of North America—the eastern United States, parts of the Southwest, and the West Coast. It is a member of the primitive marsupial group, which also includes the Australian kangaroo and the koala bear. (Harold W. Hoffman)

within the uterus. The most commonly known marsupials are found today in Australia, where there are few placental mammals. There are Australian marsupials that resemble rabbits, squirrels, mice, cats, dogs, and anteaters, although the best-known are unique—the kangaroo and the koala bear (which is not a bear at all). Marsupials once lived all over the world, but few species exist outside Australia now; one of these is North American, the Virginia opossum, which is still much the same as it was 100 million years ago. Like other marsupials, the female opossum gives birth to tiny, immature young, often as many as a dozen, less than two weeks after conception. The embryonic opossums, clinging to their mother's fur, crawl up her abdomen to the pouch, where they attach themselves to her nipples. They remain there for about two months. Once the babies emerge from the pouch, complete with fur coats and long tails like the adult opossum, they will stick close to their

Shrews are tiny animals that resemble the earliest-known mammals that existed at the same time as the dinosaurs. This pygmy shrew is the smallest mammal in all of North America, weighing in at only one-eighth of an ounce. (Stephen Dalton)

mother, riding on her back or hanging on to her tail as she moves.

When the young opossums move out on their own, they learn to feed on a variety of things—insects, worms, berries, fruit, corn, and whatever meat they can find, including birds, snakes, frogs, and other mammals. Opossums like to eat carrion, especially in the form of road-killed animals, which often results in their becoming victims of automobiles themselves.

Adult opossums are both solitary and nocturnal, and they have two effective defense mechanisms to ward off danger. The first is a formidable set of fifty teeth, which they will display with a fierce hiss when threatened. The second is a tendency to roll over as if dead—*playing possum*—until the attacker moves away. Although the opossum will hole up for several days in cold weather, it does not truly hibernate. Females will use a nest in a hollow log or an empty burrow to raise litters of young opossums as often as two or three times a year. The full-grown opossum is about the size of a large domestic cat and has an opposable thumb (like a human's) and a prehensile tail (like a

monkey's), which it uses to cling to branches or carry its babies.

THE INSECT EATERS

Another very ancient group of mammals is the order known as insectivores, or insect eaters, which in North America includes shrews and moles. Animals very like these lived alongside the dinosaurs hundreds of millions of years ago and somehow managed to survive in spite of the extraordinary odds against them. Insectivores have small brains and are not very intelligent; their eyesight is poor; they are very small, timid, and comparatively defenseless. But like the synapsids of long ago, they are exceptionally alert and sensitive in spite of their small size. Shrews, unlike mice, have tiny ears, but they have excellent hearing and are very nervous and active, which helps them both to avoid their enemies and to catch their food. To maintain their high metabolism—that is, the rate at which they turn food into energy—shrews must eat every three hours or so and often consume as much as twice their weight in food each day.

Insects are their principal diet, but they will also eat plants and even other small mammals, which they can paralyze with a poison in their saliva. Shrews are hunted by many larger animals. An odor produced by their musk glands makes them unappetizing to many animals, but not to owls and snakes, for which they are an important source of food. Shrews tend to be solitary—although mates will occasionally form strong bonds—and they defend their territories with great ferocity. The average shrew lives less than a year in nature, but within that time the female may produce as many as four litters of five to seven babies. One curious bit of behavior that seems to be unique to shrews occurs when the young are disturbed. A noise or even a change in weather will cause each shrew in the litter to grasp the tail of the one in front so that the group, led by the mother, forms a tiny procession, which will move for some distance, presumably to safety.

Moles are less vulnerable than shrews, because they live almost entirely in burrows, which they make with their enlarged forefeet so quickly that they can move through soft earth at about one foot per minute. They are streamlined in shape, and their velvety-soft fur enables them to move easily forward or backward in their tunnels. Although their ears are hidden in their fur (which keeps them from becoming clogged with dirt), moles can hear well. Their eyesight is very poor, but their noses and whiskers are extremely sensitive to smell and to vibrations in the earth. Gardeners often think of moles as terrible pests because their burrows create mounds in otherwise perfect lawns, but in fact moles perform a valuable anti-erosion service by aerating the earth and allowing rain to penetrate. And, of course, like shrews, moles dine mainly on insects, which is beneficial to humans as well. Unlike shrews, moles have only one litter a year, but they don't have as much reason to rush through life, since they can live up to five years in the wild at a much more leisurely pace.

THE ARMORED MAMMALS

Like shrews and moles, armored mammals are a very old group of animals that has managed to survive in spite of competition from more advanced mammals. This group,

which includes anteaters, sloths, and armadillos, once existed only in South America, but one species, the nine-banded armadillo, has gradually moved north and is now relatively common in the southern United States. Although this group, called the edentate group, is not highly evolved in terms of intelligence, its members are very specialized in certain ways that have enabled them to maintain their unique place in nature. (The word *edentate*, incidentally, means *toothless*, but only the anteater actually has no teeth. The giant armadillo of South America, for instance, has as many as a hundred!)

What sets the armadillo apart from other mammals is its calcified leatherlike skin that is constructed rather like a suit of armor, each plate on its back connected to the next by soft, flexible skin. Like armor, this unusual hide works as a defense mechanism, for when the armadillo is threatened, it can safely crawl into thorny bushes where predators cannot follow, or if no refuge is in sight, it can roll itself into a ball to protect its tender underbelly. Although the armadillo can also use its powerful front claws in self-defense, it is a timid animal and prefers to use its claws for digging, which it does very well and quickly, creating instant burrows where it will build a nest for raising its young.

Because armadillos need to live where the earth can be easily burrowed, they are abundant in sandy areas and along streams, where they feed by nosing around for insects, a few edible plants, and the occasional small mammal or amphibian. They look clumsy in motion, but they can perform some remarkable athletic feats, such as walking underwater for as long as ten minutes or inflating their lungs to stay buoyant while swimming. One of the animal's most intriguing characteristics is that the female armadillo gives birth once a year to four identical babies, which are capable of walking in only a few hours. Because their armor is still soft, the youngsters stay with their mother for a few weeks until they can manage on their own. Armadillos can live as long as seven years in the wild, although they are often prey to hunters and to automobiles, against which their armor affords no protection at all.

Although moles have very poor eyesight, their senses of smell and touch are highly developed. The star-nosed mole is remarkably sensitive, using its tentacles to find its way through its burrow in search of food. (Rod Planck)

The eastern or common mole lives almost all of its life underground and can move very quickly through its tunnel either forward or backward. (Gregory K. Scott)

RODENTS
AND THEIR RELATIVES

The mountain beaver is not a beaver but a primitive species of rodent native to the American West, where it burrows in forested areas.
(Tom McHugh; see page 24.)

Rodents make up the largest mammalian order, including nearly three thousand species or almost half of the mammal species in the world. They are among the most successful animals on earth, having been able to adapt to just about every type of habitat, including man's. Their success is largely due to their diversity and adaptability. In North America alone, rodents range from the tiny harvest mouse to the large beaver, including species that are able to swim, run, climb, burrow, and even glide through the air. Some rodents are capable of hibernating in winter (or estivating in summer) when the weather and lack of vegetation make it difficult for them to survive: The animal's body tem-

perature is reduced to conserve energy, enabling it to sleep through the winter or summer without eating. Like the shrews and other small animals, rodents expend a lot of energy maintaining their body heat when awake and must eat large quantities of food every day. What sets rodents apart from the other mammals is their remarkable teeth, which include two pairs of incisors that grow throughout life; these incisors are worn down and sharpened as the animal gnaws. Rodents can cause a great deal of damage by chewing property or stored food, and many of them carry diseases that are harmful to man, so they are considered by many to be terrible pests. A number of rodents, however, have proved invaluable to us, since they keep insects and weeds under control, and, of course, millions of domesticated rodents are used every year in medical research.

This eastern chipmunk, one of twenty species of chipmunks native to North America, is a small, attractive member of the squirrel family.
(Stephen Maslowski; see page 24.)

Belding's ground squirrel, a native of the American West, hibernates in winter for as long as eight months. It lives in large colonies, and families may live for many generations in the same area. (M. J. Griffith)

The woodchuck, a large member of the squirrel family, is a common garden pest in cultivated areas, but in nature it prefers to feed on lichen and other wild vegetation. (Gaston Lepage)

THE MOUNTAIN BEAVER

The sewellel or mountain beaver, which is not actually a beaver at all, is the most primitive rodent species, not closely related to the other families of rodents in existence today. It looks like a muskrat or a woodchuck and lives in the forests of the Pacific Northwest and parts of Nevada, where it makes intricate burrow systems that include sleeping nests and separate chambers for storing food and for depositing "garbage." These tunnels, which are close to the surface of the earth, are often used by other animals, including weasels and minks, which are the mountain beaver's primary enemies. Mountain beavers eat mostly grass, ferns, and tree bark, although they will occasionally gnaw on small limbs, which is probably why they are called beavers. Because they must keep their teeth trim and sharp, they also use rocks or lumps of clay for gnawing; these objects, called "mountain beaver baseballs," can be found in special rooms in their burrows or serving as doors for vacated areas. Like many rodents, these animals are mostly nocturnal, but they will sometimes browse during the day for food, especially in cool weather, and they never stray far from home. The annual litter of four or five babies is born in the spring and weaned in the fall.

THE SQUIRREL FAMILY

This is one of the largest rodent groups and includes many more creatures than the familiar gray squirrel seen so often in parks and backyards. Woodchucks, chipmunks, marmots, and prairie dogs are all squirrels, too, though they hardly deserve the family name Sciuridae, which means "shade tail" and refers to the squirrel's long bushy tail that is sometimes used to shield the body from weather. Nevertheless, the tail is an important part of every squirrel, even if not always used as an umbrella. Most squirrels spend a great deal of time in trees, and the tail is very helpful in maintaining balance; flying squirrels use them as rudders, and the grounded squirrels—from chipmunks to the woodchuck—use them as props for sitting up straight while they survey their surroundings.

There are at least twenty species of chipmunks in North America, and all of them are similar in appearance—small, striped, bushy-tailed, with bright dark eyes—and are very alert. They spend most of their time on the ground, although they can climb trees if necessary, and they feed mainly on nuts, seeds, fruits, and berries, though some spice up their diet with insects, flowers, and fungi. They will usually stockpile food for the winter; in fact, they seem to be constantly collecting food and storing it. During the winter, chipmunks in cold regions will hibernate for several months, waking occasionally for a snack. All but one of the American chipmunks live in the West, preferring all sorts of forested areas from the mountains to the lowlands. The characteristic striping on their backs serves as protective coloration in the underbrush where they are active much of the day. It is interesting to note that the yellow-pine chipmunk, which lives in open forests, has well-defined stripes that resemble sun-cast shadows, while the Sonoma chipmunk has indistinct stripes, more appropriate for dense underbrush. Chipmunks are very vocal, with high-pitched rapid calls of various types; "chip-chip" is most common and obviously what gave them their name.

Ground squirrels look much like chipmunks except that most species have no stripes. In North America they are found west of the Mississippi, inhabiting open meadows and prairies as well as forested areas, relying more on burrows than on coloration for protection. Ground squirrels hibernate longer than most other animals, going underground as early as midsummer and remaining there until the first signs of spring. They are quite gregarious, often living in large colonies, and they spend much of the day searching for seeds and other food or sunning themselves. Ground squirrels are very alert and when alarmed will dive into their burrows for safety.

In both appearance and behavior, marmots and prairie dogs are like large ground squirrels. They climb trees only when they have to and spend most of their time on the ground in open country, where they feed on plant materials, stuffing themselves in autumn to accumulate fat in order to hibernate through the winter. Marmots are relatively large—up to thirty inches long, including the tail—and tend to be fairly solitary, unlike ground squirrels. One species of marmot is the woodchuck, which, true to its

This prairie dog is also a member of the squirrel family. It uses its sturdy tail to sit up by its burrow to survey the vast open plains of the Midwest, where it lives.
(Stephen J. Krasemann)

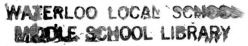

A close relative of the common gray squirrel, this fox squirrel of the eastern United States is larger and comes in three different colors—gray, rust, and black. (Harold W. Hoffman)

Prairie dogs live in the grasslands of the Midwest, and they serve as a good example of the disruption that humans have caused by interfering with nature's ecological balance. In the nineteenth century, man nearly wiped out the vast herds of bison (or buffalo), and as a result, the population of prairie dogs grew tremendously, thriving on the grass that had once supported the bison. Because the prairies were then taken over by farmers and ranchers who felt that prairie dogs were destroying crops and competing with their livestock, an extermination campaign was waged and nearly 90 percent of the prairie dogs were killed off, which in turn led to diminished numbers of black-footed ferrets, their primary predator. Nowadays, the farmers realize that prairie dogs can actually help improve the land by fertilizing and aerating it, so they are now allowed to maintain their towns; their population is kept in check by controlled hunting and by natural predators, such as foxes, badgers, coyotes, and birds of prey.

Tree squirrels are very common throughout North America, and they are more easily seen than most other rodents because they remain active all year throughout the day. They dig tunnels in which they store nuts, but they make their sleeping nests or dens in trees, using hollows in winter and leafy nests in summer. They often produce two litters a year, one in early spring and the other in midsummer. While the gray squirrel is the most common tree squirrel, the tufted-ear squirrel of the Southwest is extremely rare. The fox squirrel, common in the East, is the largest American squirrel (weighing up to thirty-eight ounces), while the red squirrel, which prefers the pine forests of Canada and the northern states, is very small, weighing eight ounces or less.

Flying squirrels are the smallest tree squirrels of all, weighing only two or three ounces, and they have adapted almost completely to life in the trees. They do not really fly, but they can glide up to a hundred yards from one branch to another, since they have a fold of skin between front and back legs that acts like a sail when their legs are outstretched. Unlike their relatives, flying squirrels will eat

name, prefers to live in the open woods (it does *not* chuck wood but prefers grass and vegetation). Also known as the groundhog, this lucky fellow is the only animal to have an American holiday named for him; Groundhog Day on February 2 is the day when, according to legend (but not naturalists), the woodchuck emerges from its den to see whether spring has come. If it sees its shadow, the story goes, it goes back into the burrow for another six weeks; if it sees no shadow, it apparently assumes that spring is near and stays aboveground. Like the other marmots, the woodchuck chirps or whistles when alarmed and is hunted by many larger animals, including man.

Prairie dogs are close relatives of the marmots, but they are very gregarious, often living in groups of several thousand animals. They dig very complex burrows, or towns, which are divided into family groups, and they can often be seen sitting up at the entrances watching for enemies.

This southern flying squirrel does not really fly, but it can glide more than eighty yards from one treetop to another. (Sturgis McKeever)

Pocket gophers, found only in the West, spend much time in their burrows searching for plants. They carry food in their cheek pouches or pockets. (Anita Este)

Kangaroo rats are neither kangaroos nor rats but are closely related to the pocket gopher. They do, however, make enormous kangaroolike leaps with their enlarged hind legs. (Russ Kinne)

insects and even meat in addition to their usual diet of seeds, nuts, and berries, and they are nocturnal, which makes them difficult to see. A light tap on a hollow tree where there is a woodpecker hole, however, will sometimes rouse a flying squirrel. They live only in the eastern and northern parts of the United States and in Canada. They store food for winter use but do not hibernate like their cousins the ground squirrels.

POCKET MAMMALS

Pocket gophers, like flying squirrels, are highly specialized rodents, having physically adapted to a particular life-style, in this case to one lived almost entirely underground. Although, like other rodents, pocket gophers feed on vegetable matter—mostly roots and tubers—and they have rodent's teeth perfectly designed for gnawing, they have developed many characteristics similar to those of moles, which are not related but live in much the same way. Their fur can lie forward or back, enabling them to move in either direction in their burrows, and they have small eyes and ears with very well-developed claws on their feet for burrowing purposes. They do not hibernate but do go into their deep burrows in wintertime and live on stored food. In their search for food they also build tunnels near the surface of the earth. The food they eat contains enough water so that they never need to take a drink. Pocket gophers are small, about ten to twelve inches long. The different species are mostly found in the West and Southwest, although there are four species found in the Southeast, three of them only in the state of Georgia. Pocket gophers tend to be solitary, even aggressive toward their own kind, but they do manage to breed once or twice a year, raising two to eleven offspring, which start burrowing even before they leave home at the age of two months.

Pocket mice, which are not true mice, and kangaroo rats, which are neither kangaroos nor rats, are quite close to pocket gophers, biologically speaking. They have cheek pouches for carrying food, and they make extensive burrows with separate rooms for sleeping, storage, and raising young. Kangaroo rats are named for their wonderful jumping ability, for which purpose they have long hind legs and wide tails. Although only twelve to fifteen inches long, they can leap nearly ten feet. They also use their legs to drum on the earth as a means of communication. All twenty-two species of kangaroo rats, like the smaller kangaroo mouse and the pocket mouse, are found west of the Mississippi, many of them in the sandy deserts of the Southwest.

RATS AND MICE

Most people think of rats and mice as terrible pests, and, in fact, they are just that in many parts of the world, carrying diseases and causing damage to all kinds of human property. One of the reasons they give us such trouble is that there are so many of them—about twelve hundred different species worldwide, with very high reproductive rates—and several species have adapted to human habitats with great success. Curiously, however, the three species most familiar to Americans are not American at all: the black rat, the Norway or brown rat, and the house mouse. All of these originated in Asia but were spread by humans to every part of the world, reaching this continent in the sixteenth century.

New World rats and mice are pests in some areas, though not nearly to the extent of the Old World species, and they share a number of other characteristics with their immigrant cousins. But our seventy native species also have some special traits of their own. Most of the animals in this group have long tails with large eyes and ears, and they use burrows, breeding throughout the year to produce several litters of two to nine young. But the range in size is great—from the quarter-ounce harvest mouse to the four-to-five-pound muskrat—and habits differ greatly as well, since this rodent family has adapted to every available habitat. Most of the mice eat seeds, but some, including the appropriately named grasshopper mouse, feed on insects as well. The rats tend to be larger than the mice, and their names reflect their particular surroundings: Rice rats live in swampy marshes, cotton rats in grassy areas, wood rats in areas where there are trees and shrubs and where they build houses of sticks and grass. The bushy-tailed wood rat is also known as the pack rat, well known throughout the Northwest for its habit of collecting objects, preferably shiny ones, and hoarding them in its huge nest. Some of the mice and rats prefer desert areas and make a fine living in and around cactus and sagebrush.

The deer mouse, common in the Midwest, feeds on many types of plants—seeds, nuts, berries, fungi, and vegetables, including even the occasional carrot. (Tom McHugh)

The desert wood rat lives on cacti as well as berries and nuts, and, like the rattlesnake with which it shares its habitat, can rattle an alarm by rubbing its tail on dried plants. (Tom McHugh)

The meadow vole uses grass as nesting material and also as food, consuming nearly its own weight in grass every day. (Tom McHugh)

The collared lemming, native to the arctic tundra, is the only rodent on our continent that turns white in winter for camouflage against the snow, like other arctic animals— the snowshoe hare and the arctic fox. (Tom McHugh)

VOLES AND LEMMINGS

Voles and lemmings are in the same family as mice and rats but have somewhat different habits. They prefer the cooler temperatures of the North and are active during the day rather than at night. Their ears and eyes are smaller and their tails are shorter, but they eat similar vegetable materials and have litters of offspring all year round. The Scandinavian lemming is famous for its mass migrations, which occur every four years or so when overpopulation forces the animals to move in search of food, stopping at nothing in their travels, including the ocean, in which most of them drown. The brown lemming of North America experiences similar overpopulation crises, but the animals migrate individually rather than in large groups.

Voles are charming little creatures with widely varied habits. The meadow vole creates an intricate system of un-

derground burrows and eats nearly its weight in grass every day to keep up the hard work—much like the shrew. The red tree vole, on the other hand, lives almost entirely in trees, usually Douglas firs, and makes large and complex nests of twigs, often with passageways and rooms for several families. The red-backed vole makes no burrow at all but uses the abandoned tunnels of other animals or aboveground runways on rocks and stumps. The woodland vole spends most of its time underground, while the water vole likes to swim and lives along riverbanks.

The muskrat is a kind of vole but is different from other voles in several respects, being quite large and having adapted to an aquatic environment. Muskrats use their tails as rudders and are excellent swimmers. They live in swamps or alongside rivers and other bodies of water, where they build burrows or houses in which to sleep and raise more muskrats. Their thick pelts are prized by furriers.

AQUATIC RODENTS

Beavers live somewhat as muskrats do but are even larger—sometimes weighing more than a hundred pounds. The beaver's flat, scaly tail is slapped on mud or water to signal alarm and assist in making huge lodges—as well as serving as a rudder while swimming. The hind feet are webbed, which enables the beaver to swim as fast as five miles per hour, and, like the muskrat, it can stay underwater for as long as fifteen minutes at a time. Unlike the muskrat, which produces several litters a year, the beaver has only one annual litter. The young are raised inside a lodge, which is often built in a pond that the beavers have created themselves by damming a stream with trees, stones, and mud. Beaver dams can be up to a hundred feet wide and can create havoc by causing floods; because of this and because beaver fur is so attractive to humans, beavers are no longer found throughout the continent as they once were, although they are now protected by law in many areas and seem to be making a comeback.

The nutria is also an aquatic rodent much trapped for its fur, but it is not native to North America. It was introduced from South America and the Caribbean by fur ranchers, and a few escaped into the swamps of Louisiana during the 1930s. Nutrias, also known as coypus, often adopt the burrows and lodges of beavers and muskrats, and they feed primarily on aquatic vegetation and grains.

THE QUILLED MAMMAL

One of the most curious rodents is the porcupine. It gnaws on vegetation like other rodents and it is quite vocal as well, but there the resemblance seems to stop. A clumsy, slow-moving animal, the porcupine has little need to scurry, since it is well equipped to defend itself with over thirty thousand quills, sharp hair growths that detach easily when they come in contact with an enemy. The quills are not thrown, but the porcupine will bristle up and slash with its tail, which can force the quills to become imbedded. Perhaps because they live as long as eight years and can de-

The beaver is much larger than the muskrat and is capable of felling sizable trees by gnawing around the bases. It cuts the trees into pieces and uses them to construct massive dams. (Pat & Tom Leeson)

The muskrat, a large member of the vole family, lives like the beaver in a watery habitat, building big houses along the banks of rivers and lakes. (Norman R. Lightfoot; see page 30.)

The nutria also lives in an aquatic environment but is not native to North America. It escaped into the wild from commercial breeding farms, where it is raised for its valuable fur. (Tom McHugh; see page 31.)

fend themselves so well, porcupines do not reproduce as prolifically as the other rodents, producing only one baby a year. Breeding is not as difficult as one might think, for the female is carefully courted by the male and can relax her quills when she is sufficiently aroused. Porcupines can swim and climb trees, which they often gnaw on during the winter months. They have a particular fondness for salt and will therefore also gnaw on ax handles and other tools that have absorbed human sweat.

FLYING MAMMALS

Although bats are often thought of as flying mice or rats, they are not rodents at all. In fact, they make up an entirely separate order—Chiroptera—that probably evolved from tree shrews and that has become the largest order of mammals after rodents. Bats are the only mammals that truly fly. The arm and finger bones are very long, and between them are thin membranes that are used as wings in flight and can be folded up at rest. The clawed hind feet are used to support the bat—upside down—when it is not flying and also to groom the fur and teeth. Bats have very poor eyesight, but their ears are so sensitive that they can find insects and avoid flying into things by echolocation—that is, by responding to sound waves that they create by making high-pitched noises that bounce off nearby objects. This form of echolocation is similar to sonar devices and to the method used by dolphins and other underwater creatures.

Bats are nocturnal and prefer dark areas for roosting—cages, burrows, barns, and hollow trees—where they form large groups, though a few species are solitary and live in trees. Bats can hibernate but will die in below-freezing temperatures, so most of them are found in warmer regions during the winter months. Most bats will avoid human contact, but still they are much feared and despised, even considered monsters. In actuality, bats successfully control the population of destructive insects and are quite harmless, except in rare cases of rabies, a disease to which all warm-blooded animals are susceptible. The fear that a

The porcupine, because of its quill-covered body, doesn't look much like its rodent relatives, but it has the same effective gnawing teeth. It lives exclusively on vegetation. (Cosmos Blank)

The vampire bat is rare in North America, but its reputation has helped to give all bats a bad name. Most bats live on insects and do far more good than harm. (William E. Townsend Jr.)

The little brown myotis bat is very common throughout the United States and like all bats is a true flier, migrating many hundreds of miles each year. (William M. Partington)

bat will fly into one's hair is based on the fact that bats do often fly close to animals in search of insects that swarm close to their heads.

Most bats live on insects, though a few prefer nectar and fruit. Vampire bats, which exist only in the western hemisphere, do suck blood, but usually from birds, although they may also attack livestock. Unlike other bats they see fairly clearly and can walk as well as fly. Fortunately for North America, there are very few that migrate north of Mexico.

The most common North American bat is probably the little brown myotis, which, like most bats, raises one youngster a year. The mother bats gather in "nursery" colonies or maternity caves, where the concentration of animals increases the temperature to help protect the newborns. The mother bat will often leave her young in search of food, but when disturbed, she will pick up the baby and carry it with her when she flies—an appealing maternal gesture for such a strange-looking creature.

THE RABBIT FAMILY

Another order of mammals often associated with rodents is the lagomorphs, which include rabbits, hares, and pikas. Like rodents, these attractive furry animals have incisor teeth that grow throughout life and must be worn down constantly to keep them trim. They are also strictly vegetarian and vulnerable to a great many predators. Unlike rodents, however, they "chew their cud"—a protective device that allows them to swallow food and run to a safe spot where they can regurgitate the food pellets for dining at leisure. Lagomorphs are very successful mammals, having adapted to many different habitats. Pikas (or conies), which resemble guinea pigs, are small, with little round ears and short hind legs. They live in rocky areas in the western part of North America, dining on green plants that they cut and dry in the sun like hay for use in the winter months. Pikas are very noisy, constantly chattering to each other in their large colonies.

Rabbits and hares are quite similar to each other, with long ears and hind legs and excellent peripheral vision that helps alert them to danger on all sides. Unlike pikas, they are mostly nocturnal and solitary, although they will warn others of danger by thumping their legs on the ground or giving a loud distress call. Hares are larger than rabbits and are generally better runners, while rabbits tend to hide in underbrush to escape predators. Presumably because they are so vulnerable, both groups are extremely prolific. It is estimated that a pair of cottontail rabbits could theoreti-

The white-tailed jackrabbit is a hare, not a rabbit, and is very common in the West and Southwest. Unlike rabbits, jackrabbits are born with full fur coats and open eyes and can fend for themselves in less than a month. (Harry Engels)

cally have as many as 350,000 descendants in five years if none died. But the death rate is high, and rabbits rarely live more than a year. Some rabbits will swim if necessary, but most prefer grassland areas, using the burrows of other animals for safety and making their nests in brush or high grass. The pygmy rabbit—the smallest on the continent—is unique in digging its own burrow. The domestic or European rabbit, which is not native, also digs burrows or warrens and has caused much destruction in farm country.

Hares do not make nests or burrows, undoubtedly relying on their speed and protective coloration. The snowshoe hare, also called the varying hare, lives in the northern half of North America and changes its hair coat from brown to white in the winter, when it serves as camouflage in the snow. Jackrabbits, which are hares, not rabbits, do not change color, since they are more common in the southern states. They are exceptionally fast, reaching thirty-five to forty miles per hour and leaping up to twenty feet at a time. The brown jackrabbit will flash its white tail and sides as it runs, which often confuses predators and may even serve to warn other jacks in the vicinity. The name comes from "jackass," because of the very large ears, although "jumping jack" would be equally appropriate.

The pika, a cousin to the rabbit and a native of the West, is a highly vocal animal, often bleating loudly like a goat to communicate with its own kind. (L. & D. Klein)

The European rabbit, as its name implies, is not a native North American but was introduced to provide a larger game species than the cottontail. Unfortunately, the effort backfired, because this rabbit is active only at night and has caused much damage in agricultural areas because of its feeding habits and extensive burrows. (Townsend P. Dickinson)

The eastern cottontail rabbit is usually seen hopping around in search of food, but it can also stand on its hind legs to get a good view of the landscape and will leap as far as fifteen feet if necessary. (John Bova)

HOOFED MAMMALS

The massive horns of the male bighorn sheep are used in butting contests to determine dominance in the herd. (Tom Branch; see page 50.)

In the previous chapter, we discussed a very large number of mammals that live almost entirely on plant material, the small rodents that have been able to adapt to nearly every possible habitat on the North American continent. In this chapter, we will meet a group of animals that share feeding habits but are otherwise much different in both behavior and appearance. Ungulates, or hoofed mammals, are much larger than the small herbivorous rodents and are primarily grazing animals, living on grasses rather than seeds or nuts or fruit. Their teeth are therefore designed somewhat differently—specialized not for gnawing but for tearing off grassy stems and grinding them. Because, like rabbits, hoofed mammals run to escape predators rather than hiding or

Although the white-tailed deer is a good runner and swimmer, it prefers to hide rather than run great distances. It is active at night and sleeps in underbrush, which provides a good cover. (Leonard Lee Rue III; see page 41.)

fighting back, many ungulates have evolved a method of feeding that enables them to eat quickly and digest at leisure: chewing the cud. This involves storing undigested food in the rumen (or first stomach), forming it into pellets (or cuds) in the second stomach, and then regurgitating them for chewing when the animal is safe from predators. Since most grasslands are relatively open, animals inhabiting them tend to live in groups and learn to run quickly as methods of defense. Incredibly, the young of most hoofed animals are ready to run within a day of being born, although the young of most other mammals are relatively helpless at birth. Ungulates tend to have good eyesight and excellent hearing, but their most unusual feature is the design of their hooves, which are specially formed toes enclosed in a horny sheath to protect them from the shock of impact as they run. There are two orders of ungulates— odd-toed and even-toed. Only the even-toed ungulates, called arteriodactyls, are naturally present in North America. (The odd-toed ungulates include the rhinoceros, tapirs, and horses, which are wild here today only because they were introduced by humans.) The even-toed ungulates include the hippopotamus, the giraffe, the gnu, the camel, and a splendid array of antelope and deer, but most of these are African. America has an impressive group as well, however, some of which are introduced—such as the wild boar and domestic cattle—and some of which are native.

WILD PIGS AND PECCARIES

The collared peccary is a relative of the domestic pig, which it resembles in many ways. Peccaries grunt while they root for food (prickly pear cactus is a favorite, since they live in the Southwest), they do not chew their cud, they squeal (though only when very upset), and they have cloven hooves and straight tusks. Peccaries, however, rarely weigh more than fifty to sixty pounds, whereas some domestic pigs can weigh hundreds of pounds. Peccaries swim well and run very fast—up to twenty-five miles per hour. They travel in herds and breed throughout the year, producing two to six offspring in a litter. The peccary can live as long as twenty years. It has several predators, including man, and its range has been reduced to parts of Arizona, New Mexico, and Texas.

The wild boar, on the other hand, a true member of the swine family but not native to North America, seems to thrive here, most likely because it is much larger, weighing up to 350 pounds, and the males are equipped with fierce tempers and long tusks, which keep predators to a minimum. In some states, wild boars are hunted by man for food or because they are considered pests in agricultural areas. In addition to roots, grass, fruits, and nuts, wild boars will eat reptiles, mice, bird eggs, carrion, and even fawns or baby rabbits. Some wild boars are actually descendants of escaped domestic pigs; others are pure-blooded European wild boars brought in by hunters to hunting preserves in the United States. Like the smaller peccaries, wild boars run in herds, which consist of sows and their young, since the males form small groups or remain solitary except during the breeding season.

A relative of the domestic pig, the collared peccary is a good runner—up to twenty-five miles per hour—and a good swimmer. It travels in herds and can live as long as twenty years. (Jan Lindblad)

THE DEER FAMILY

Although there is a good deal of difference in size and behavior between the moose and the white-tailed deer, all members of the deer family have much in common. Most male deer (and the female caribou) grow antlers each year, and in all species the does are smaller than the males. The antlers usually start growing in late spring, beginning in yearling bucks with straight spikes and branching out and increasing in size and complexity each year until maturity. Antlers are bony outgrowths of the front of the skull. They are rather soft at first and are covered with short hairs or "velvet," which contains blood vessels that nourish the antlers; later, the velvet dries up and falls off (or else is scraped off), and the males use the bare antlers to attract mates and to discourage rivals during the breeding season, after which the entire antler is shed.

The white-tailed deer is the most common deer in the United States (it also ranges into southern Canada but is not found in California or the Southwest). Though it was once seriously threatened in certain areas, it is very abundant now, thanks to hunting restrictions and the lack of natural predators. The name comes from the deer's habit of raising its tail when alarmed, showing the white beneath, which serves to alert other deer and makes it easier for a fawn to follow its running mother. The fawn—or two, since older does will often have twins or even triplets if food is plentiful—will stay with its mother for a year or more. Fawns are spotted, which helps to camouflage them in foliage. Males and females usually separate during the spring and summer but may herd together in winter. These deer feed on grass and other plants during the summer but will eat nuts in the fall and browse on trees and shrubs in winter. They are active mostly at night but can often be seen during the day, especially at dawn or twilight. White-tailed deer vary in size depending on their range and the availability of food; most are three to three and a half feet tall at the shoulder and weigh from 150 pounds (females) to 300 pounds (males), but the tiny Key deer, a subspecies that lives in the Florida Keys and was once seriously en-

The mule deer, a native of the western United States and Canada, is named for its exceptionally large ears, which move constantly as it listens for its enemies.
(Jerry L. Ferrara)

dangered, is only two feet tall and weighs about 50 pounds.

The mule deer and its close relative the black-tailed deer are found only in the western states. Like the white-tailed deer, they are good swimmers and can run up to thirty-five miles per hour, though not for long distances. Since they live in mountainous areas and forests rather than open farmland, they will eat berries as well as plants and they like evergreens in the winter. Mule deer will migrate down mountains in the winter but seldom herd up except in winter.

The elk or wapiti is a much larger deer; males can weigh up to a thousand pounds and females up to six hundred. It once had a range over most of the United States and south-

ern Canada, but it was hunted heavily and is now restricted principally to the northwestern states and parts of Canada. Much of its original range included the prairies of the Midwest, where it developed a taste for grasses rather than other vegetation, although it will feed on wood and lichens in winter. Female elk, or cows, will also travel in large herds led by a single bull; generally speaking, the more open the country, the larger the herds. Elk are highly vocal, snorting and bugling and even whistling, most often during the breeding season.

The moose, which is known as an elk in Europe, is the largest of all the deer, males weighing up to eighteen hundred pounds. The antlers are very broad and flat and may span nearly six feet. The muzzle is large, and there is a dewlap beneath the chin. Like all deer, moose are good swimmers, but they spend more time than the others near water, where they feed on aquatic plants and wallow in mud to fend off biting insects. In winter, they browse in marshy

Although the elk is much larger than the white-tailed deer and not nearly so graceful in appearance, it can move much more quietly through the woods, even at high speeds.
(F. B. Grunzweig)

Caribou, which are members of the deer family, are also known in Europe as reindeer. They migrate over long distances in the spring. (Stephen J. Krasemann)

The pronghorn is one of the fastest animals in the world and can maintain a speed of thirty-five miles per hour for as long as fifteen minutes. Their sharp hooves are effective weapons if they are forced to fight. (Alan Carey; see page 49.)

forests on aspen, birch, and other deciduous trees. Moose tend to be solitary during the warm months, but the bulls will begin to join the females in late summer for the breeding season, and herds are often formed in winter. Both cows and bulls will bellow during the breeding season, and though moose generally shy from humans, males are aggressive at this time and cows become quite fierce when their calves are born in the spring.

Caribou are the same species as the domestic reindeer of northern Europe. Although they are true deer, their behavior is quite unlike that of the other species. They are not solitary but travel in large groups—often as many as 100,000 together—and will migrate long distances before the calves are born in spring and during the fall before

The male musk-ox is a relatively solitary animal except during the breeding season, when he joins the herds of females and young. (Kenneth W. Fink; see page 50.)

The bison, the largest land animal in
North America, was once also one of
the most numerous. Bison are
restricted to special areas in the United States
as a means of protection, but in Canada they
run free, making migrations of a hundred miles or
more between summer and winter ranges,
as they once did on the North American prairies.
(Tom McHugh)

breeding. Like moose, caribou range over much of Canada, but they prefer treeless tundra to forest and in winter will feed on lichens as well as other types of vegetation. Because of their inclination for travel, caribou are especially swift—reaching speeds of fifty miles per hour for short distances—and their flat, hairy feet are adapted for walking over wet tundra in summer and over snow in winter.

THE PRONGHORN

The pronghorn has, as its name suggests, a set of horns rather than antlers. The horns grow throughout life; their sheath of keratin (similar to a human fingernail) is shed each year, but the horns remain. Because of these horns it is often called the American antelope, though in fact it is not an antelope. It is unique in another important way—it is the fastest mammal in North America, capable of speeds of up to seventy miles per hour. Not surprisingly, this speedy creature lives in open plains, grazing in summer and browsing in winter, mostly on sagebrush, since its range includes much of the Southwest as well as the Midwest. At one time, pronghorns were almost as numerous as bison and like them were hunted nearly to extinction by farmers who felt that they competed with livestock for food. Their number also declined because of the fencing of open grasslands, which, since they cannot jump fences, prevented them from migrating. Like other open-land animals, pronghorns tend to travel in herds, usually led by a male, and are well adapted to their terrain. They have good peripheral vision for spotting danger, and when alarmed they raise the white hairs on the rump patch, alerting other pronghorns.

WILD COWS AND SHEEP

The bovine family includes many types of domestic cows, goat, and sheep, but there are some wild North American species that are truly remarkable in many ways. The most impressive in both history and appearance is the bison, or American buffalo, the largest land animal on the continent, with males weighing up to a ton. The bison prefers the open plains and prairies of the Midwest, though it can also be found in forested areas. Like pronghorns, bison were once extremely numerous in their range. It is estimated that in the fifteenth century, before the arrival of Europeans, there were some 60 million bison in North America, while in 1900 there were less than a thousand. This severe decline in numbers came about partly as the result of deliberate extinction in order to subdue the Indians and partly as a source of meat, hide, bone (for bone china), and sport. Thanks to conservation efforts, the present population of captive and free-roaming bison is now more than thirty thousand—still far short of the original figure and restricted to a much smaller range. The bison originally migrated north and south with the seasons to feed on grass, but now they are kept in isolated preserves to prevent epidemics and to control breeding. Males and females tend to stay in separate herds except during the summer breeding season; offspring stay with their mothers until they are sexually mature—at age three for females and at five for males. Like other herd animals found on open range, bison can run fast, up to thirty-five miles per hour, and they also swim well. They are very vocal, snorting and bellowing during the breeding season, when they can be heard for miles around.

The musk-ox, biologically speaking, falls somewhere between being a cow and a sheep. The "musk" in the name refers to the male's very strong odor, which is not truly musk but comes from its strong urine scent. The male musk-ox may weigh as much as nine hundred pounds, the female up to seven hundred, and both sexes have massive horns. Females and their young live in herds, while the males remain separate except for breeding in summer; they do not migrate great distances but will move from the summer range in meadows and valleys of the arctic tundra to the mountainsides in winter, where vegetation is exposed. Although they can run well, musk-oxen have developed a method of defending themselves against predators such as wolves by forming a circle or line in front of their young and even attacking their enemies, crushing them with hooves and horns.

The mountain goat, which is not a member of the goat family but of a special group of goat-antelopes, is also a northern mammal, preferring mountainous areas above the treeline in Alaska, the northwestern United States, and western Canada. They migrate up and down mountains following vegetation and are exceptionally agile, with hooves that grip well on steep and smooth rocky surfaces. Mountain goat kids are often born on ledges, and they spend their lives moving along sheer cliffs. Falls and rockslides are more

dangerous to them than are predators, which are wary of the mountain goat's sharp hooves. Males and females tend to stay in separate herds until the late fall, when they breed. Mountain goats are white, with short horns, creating a spectacular appearance on mountainsides but blending into the snowy landscape when necessary.

The bighorn sheep, also called the mountain sheep, is a remarkable climber, too, with hooves that provide good traction on rocks, but it ranges much farther south than the mountain goat, from southwestern Canada to the southwestern states, and it prefers foothills and mountain meadows to cliffs. This sheep is a grazing animal, feeding on grasses in summer and on shrubs and trees in winter. The bighorn sheep has a magnificent pair of curling horns. The males use their horns to butt each other during the breeding season, charging each other at great speed and making a resounding crack that will echo for quite a distance. Most of the year the bighorns travel in small groups of females and young, the rams joining them only in winter. Bighorns are brown, with a predominantly white rump patch, unlike their relative the dall sheep, which is usually all white and native to northwestern Canada and Alaska. Dall sheep also have butting contests and exhibit other types of bighorn behavior. Although both species have many predators, including eagles, bears, wolves, and wild cats, they are very agile and wary, so adult bighorns rarely fall prey to these enemies. Because of hunting, however, as well as man's invasion of their habitat, the bighorn population is only 1 percent of what it once was—down from 2 million to twenty thousand in only a century.

The mountain goat is completely at home in its rocky habitat, migrating up and down mountains in search of food with incredible surefootedness, even on icy cliffs.
(Leonard Lee Rue III)

PREDATORY MAMMALS

The river otter is a relative of the weasel but has a far more agreeable nature. It plays in and around the water where it makes its home. (Jeanne White; see page 64.)

Many of the mammals we have met so far have much in common: They live on plants rather than living creatures and they spend a great deal of time avoiding their enemies by one means or another. In this chapter, we will be introduced to the enemies—the predatory mammals that make their living by hunting and dining on other animals. Unappealing as that sounds, this order of mammals—the carnivores, or meat eaters—is one with which we humans can readily identify, because carnivores' brains are well developed, like ours, and because they share our methods of raising young as well as our habits of feeding on meat.

Unlike the rodents, which reproduce frequently and in great numbers, carnivores are relatively scarce, producing few young each year; unlike hoofed mammals, carnivores

The ocelot, a small spotted cat that climbs and swims as well as it runs, is an endangered species that is only rarely seen in the American Southwest. (Jan Lindblad; see page 75.)

are mostly solitary and their offspring are helpless at birth and need to be nurtured for a long time and taught to fend for themselves. Although the population of some carnivores has been severely affected by human interference—leading to near extinction in some (the wolf, the grizzly bear, and the black-footed ferret) and to overpopulation in others (the raccoon and coyote)—carnivores have always been fewer in number than the species on which they prey. This is primarily because carnivores exist at the top of the food chain, where there is little room for many animals. The food chain begins with the energy that comes from the sun and is absorbed by plant life, which in turn passes the energy along to the plant eaters. When these animals are eaten by the carnivores, the available energy has been reduced so that it can support only a few animals rather than a great many. When you consider the fact that the average carnivore will expend most of its energy in finding, hunting, and killing its prey, you can see that carnivores' lives are tenuous and difficult at best.

In the past, humans have thought of the carnivorous animals as bloodthirsty killers, aggressive and fearsome—and to a limited extent this is true, since they survive by killing—but in recent years we have begun to understand the importance of predatory animals in the environment and their necessary role in controlling and even improving the populations of prey species. Wolves, for example, rarely attack full-grown, healthy caribou (or humans, for that matter); a fast-running, sharp-hoofed caribou would be both difficult to catch and dangerous to attack, so the wolves prefer to take the sick, disabled, old, or very young members of the herd, which in the long run helps keep the herd strong rather than weakening it. Wolves live and hunt in groups, but most other carnivores prefer to live a solitary life—except when breeding or raising young—and they often need large territories of their own in which they have exclusive hunting rights, so to speak. When there are too many carnivores competing for the same food, they all do badly—prey and predator alike—and when there are too few carnivores, the prey species can explode to unmanageable proportions, as one occasionally sees with rabbits, rodents, and even deer.

Not all carnivores live on meat alone; many of them, including bears and raccoons, will eat fruits and plants as well, being omnivorous, like humans. Although most carnivores are fairly large (they must be, in order to subdue their prey, unless they work in groups, as the wolves do), some are small, such as the least weasel, which is less than four inches long (not including its tail). But in spite of the differences, most carnivores share the same wariness, especially of man, who is their only major predator, and the same ability to adapt to the life-styles of their prey, learning to burrow underground, climb trees, or swim, as the case may be. They are alert and intelligent, and—for most people—they are the most admired members of the animal kingdom. We covet their fur, we feel affection for their babies, and we domesticate their cousins as our household pets.

The raccoon can often be seen washing food in water before eating, not actually to clean the food but only to inspect it, since the water makes its paws more sensitive. (Phil A. Dotson; see page 56.)

The ringtail, a catlike member of the raccoon family, has a long tail, retractable claws, and a distinct taste for rodents. It sleeps by day in a nest on the ground but is an excellent climber and will take to the trees when hunting or hunted. (R. J. Erwin; see page 56.)

THE RING-TAILED RASCALS

One of the most appealing groups of carnivores is the procyonid family, of which the raccoon is the prominent member. All three of the species in North America are omnivorous, clever, gregarious, and adorned with bushy ringed tails.

The ringtail—which is also known as the cacomistle or miner's cat—has an especially long tail and a catlike body, and it resembles a cat in its ability to catch rodents, though it also eats insects, small reptiles, and berries. It is nocturnal, like the raccoon, and sleeps during the day in a den padded with leaves or other vegetation. When active, however, the ringtail is a real athlete, climbing trees with its very sharp claws and making spectacular leaps. The name "miner's cat" comes from the fact that ringtails were used by miners to keep rodents under control; another nickname, "civet cat," comes from the animal's ability to secrete a musky fluid from its anal glands when threatened, as does the African civet cat. The ringtail exists only in the western hemisphere, however, and in North America is found in the southwestern states and in parts of California and southern Oregon.

The raccoon is larger and not so active. It has a distinctive black face mask to go with its ringed tail. This mischievous appearance is matched by a pair of nimble front paws that can open door latches and garbage cans with great ease; raccoons have adapted well to human surroundings, and they are often considered pests in residential areas, having lost their fear of humans. A full-grown raccoon can be quite aggressive, however, and is a fierce fighter, so one should avoid confronting it directly. Raccoons are also omnivorous, living on insects, fruit, rodents, eggs, and baby birds; since they are good swimmers, they will also eat aquatic animals, including frogs and fish, and they can often be found near woodland streams. Although much hunted for their fur and for sport, raccoons are so adaptable that their numbers have never been seriously threatened; if anything, they seem to thrive on their contact with humans. They are common all over the United States, and they may hole up in a den during the coldest months, although they do not truly hibernate.

The coati is more common in South America, but is found in parts of Arizona, New Mexico, and Texas. Coatis resemble raccoons but are slimmer, with small dark feet and a long mobile nose that they poke into leaves for insects; they will also eat fruit, of which they are especially fond. Unlike the raccoon, which is relatively solitary except during breeding season or when raising young, coatis often travel in bands of six to several dozen. They are active during the day, though they will sleep during the hot midday, and they are quite noisy—chattering and whining and grunting as they play and forage. Coatis swim well and climb trees extremely well, using their tails for balance. Like other members of the procyonid family and like cats, they spend a good deal of the time grooming themselves, "combing" their fur and teeth with their claws and otherwise keeping themselves clean and handsome. It is undoubtedly their attractive appearance, as well as their cleverness, that has caused some people to want to make pets of them, but they can be destructive and even aggressive if frightened, so they aren't ideal for most human households.

THE BAD-TEMPERED BUNCH

The weasel family, known as the mustelids, is large and varied and, for the most part, given to behavior and traits that humans tend to find unappealing, including a strong odor and an aggressive disposition. Although they can be destructive to poultry and have been hunted as pests as well as for their fur, these animals do serve to control rodents and insects very effectively, and they do far more good to farmers than harm. Their odor, secreted by anal scent glands, is used for defense by the skunk, but most members of the family use it as a means of communicating with one another, either marking territories or attracting mates.

There are three North American members of the weasel family that are actually called weasels—the least weasel, ounce for ounce the toughest carnivore on the continent as well as the smallest; the short-tailed weasel, also known as the stoat or ermine; and the long-tailed weasel. All three species are brown during the summer months but turn white in winter in the northern part of their range, although their tails remain black. The long-tailed weasel is

The black-footed ferret is exceptionally rare, since humans have seriously depleted its main source of food, the prairie dog. Conservationists are trying to save the ferret, a relative of the European ferret, which is sometimes kept in this country as a pet. (Stephen J. Krasemann; see page 58.)

native to most of the United States, while the other two prefer to live in Canada and the northern states only. Weasels live entirely on meat, and they are expert hunters, pouncing on animals that often are larger than they are—which accounts for their extraordinary aggressiveness—and killing in one quick bite. They are extremely agile and lithe and can work their way into narrow burrows or holes in search of mice, their favorite food, though they also prey on shrews, moles, and even baby birds. They prefer open woodlands and fields and will make dens in the burrows of other animals where they raise their young. The least weasel may have two or three litters a year, unusual for a carnivore, but the larger weasels have only one. As in some other mammals, the implantation of the fertilized egg in the uterus can be delayed for weeks, so that the young are not born until nearly a year after breeding, even though gestation itself is only a month long. Weasels are primarily nocturnal, but also can be seen during the day endlessly hunting for their next meal.

The black-footed ferret, a cousin of the European ferret or polecat, is somewhat larger than the weasels but has the same ability to chase rodents into their burrows. It once ranged throughout the Midwest and West and as far north as Alaska, but it has been severely reduced in numbers because of the widespread extermination of prairie dogs, its favorite prey. Ferrets like to live right in the prairie dog town, in fact, close to their food supply, and will often take over a victim's burrow, enlarging it and otherwise making it habitable. Efforts are being made now to study the behavior of the ferret and increase its population, but for the foreseeable future, this animal will remain on the endangered-species list.

The marten, weighing in at one to three pounds, is larger than the weasels and is found mostly in Canada and the

The least weasel is the smallest weasel in North America; it is in fact the smallest carnivore as well and one of the most aggressive, though it weighs less than two ounces. (Stephen Collins)

The marten, a predatory animal, is active throughout the winter months. (Russ Kinne)

Minks are valued for their beautiful fur, but they are exceptionally bad-tempered and can produce an odor nearly as strong as a skunk's, although they cannot spray it as far. When happy, which is not often, they have been known to purr.
(Stephen J. Krasemann)

northern states, where it lives in pine forests on a diet of squirrels, rabbits, and mice, though it will also eat berries, eggs, and nuts. Martens are excellent climbers and spend much of their time in trees, assisted by their strong claws and long bushy tails. Martens are most active at night and all winter long, though they do not change color as the weasels do. Their rich brown fur is extremely valuable, and they have been trapped out of much of their original range, though they are now protected by law.

The fisher is similar in appearance but much larger, up to three feet long and weighing nearly twenty pounds, and it spends more time on the ground than the marten, which occupies much of the same range. It feeds primarily on porcupines and hares, although it will also take mice and squirrels and even eat some plants. The mink is a far more common animal, ranging through most of Canada and the United States, except for the Southwest, preferring rivers and marshes to dense forest and dining on fish, frogs, turtles, and water birds, as well as rodents. Minks will often den in a muskrat burrow or dig their own den in a riverbank. They are very hostile by nature, even to each other, and will fight ferociously if their territory is invaded. And, needless to say, the mink is considered a valuable furbearer, although most commercial mink comes from ranch-raised animals. Minks use their scent glands to mark territories, as other mustelids do, and they use them in defense as well. Like other relatively small members of the weasel family, they, too, have their enemies—owls, foxes, wild cats, and hawks.

One member of the mustelid family that has little need

The wolverine, native to the forests of Canada and parts of the northwestern states, is often called the skunk bear, since it resembles a bear in shape. It is much smaller, however, yet so aggressive that it can sometimes drive a bear away from its food. (Tom McHugh)

The badger will not run very fast but it can dig burrows very quickly, thanks to the large claws on its forefeet.
(Stephen J. Krasemann)

to worry about being preyed on is the wolverine, well known for its extraordinary power and ferocity. A relatively small animal weighing between twenty and forty pounds, the wolverine is nonetheless capable of killing a large moose weakened by illness or starvation or caught in deep snow. It prefers to eat carrion and will even drive much larger predators away from kills. Also known as the "glutton," the wolverine eats voraciously, and what it cannot eat or drag away to its den it will mark with its scent, which will keep other animals away. The wolverine is native to northern Canada and appears in the United States only in the Northwest; since it requires a very large territory—as much as a thousand square miles—it is difficult to find, which, considering its temperament, is probably just as well.

The badger is also bad-tempered, but it isn't nearly as aggressive as its wolverine cousin, preferring to back down rather than fight. Protected by its thick fur and skin, sharp claws, formidable teeth, and musky odor, the badger is rarely attacked by other animals, except man, and is best

known for its digging ability, making burrows and chasing after the small rodents on which it feeds. It is especially fond of rattlesnake meat and seems to be impervious to the snake's venom. In winter the badger remains inside its deep den, sleeping for long periods—though not actually hibernating—and dining on stored food. In summer badgers will swim in cool streams, but they usually prefer open meadows and farmland. They are found in the western half of the United States and parts of southern Canada.

Although all members of the weasel family are well equipped to defend themselves, perhaps the most effective defense mechanism is that of the skunk, which is well known for its ability to spray a strongly scented musk at anything that threatens it. The hog-nosed skunk is native to Texas and the Southwest, as is the hooded skunk. The eastern spotted skunk of the Midwest and Southeast and

The striped skunk is a familiar sight throughout the United States and southern Canada, and it is one that most people try to avoid, given the skunk's ability to spray its foul-smelling musk on anyone who disturbs it. (Leonard Lee Rue III)

the striped skunk, native to most of the United States and southern Canada, are relatively widespread and common. All of the skunks are primarily black with white spots or stripes that make them quite obvious to any comers, who would be well advised to stay away! Only the great horned owl seems capable of swooping down and carrying off young skunks without getting sprayed. Skunks themselves feed on small rodents and insects, but they will also eat vegetation, including fruits and corn. They search for food primarily at night, sleeping during the day in dens, where they will also spend days at a time during the winter when the weather is particularly cold. In northern regions, skunks will eat a great deal in the autumn in order to fatten themselves up for the lean months ahead, though they do not hibernate. It is unpleasant to find oneself on the wrong side of a skunk, but more than that, they can be deadly to other mammals, including man, since they are the primary carriers of rabies in the United States.

The otters are perhaps the most appealing members of the weasel family, not just for their elegant thick fur but for their personalities. It has been said that of all animals, otters are the most playful; certainly they seem to enjoy themselves a great deal as they slide and dive and play in the water, to which they have adapted very well. Both North American species, the river otter and the sea otter, have a streamlined body with thick fur, strong tapered tail, and webbed feet, and the ears and nose have valves to keep water out. They swim extremely fast, dive brilliantly, and can remain underwater for several minutes. The river otter lives alongside streams or lakes throughout much of northern Canada, Alaska, and parts of the northwestern and southeastern states, digging burrows into the bank with doors both above and below water. The sea otter, on the other hand, lives almost entirely in salt water, off the western coast of the United States and Canada, sleeping, eating, and breeding without going on land. Both species feed

The sea otter is larger than its river relative and lives almost entirely in salt water. It can survive in cold water because its fur traps air that acts to insulate and buoy up the animal's slender body. (Karl W. Kenyon)

The coyote, which is similar in many ways to the wolf, somehow manages to thrive in spite of human efforts to wipe it out. Like many social animals, the coyote is highly vocal, howling or "singing" to communicate with its own kind. (Paul A. Johnsgard; see page 68.)

on fish, although the river otter will also eat small mammals and the sea otter loves shellfish, having developed a method of breaking shells by using rocks as tools. Since both otters have beautiful fur, they have been heavily trapped, and their numbers have also been reduced in recent years by pollution, though efforts are being made to protect them.

THE CANINE CLAN

A dog may be man's best friend, but wild members of the canid family have not always enjoyed that status. The wolf has been feared and misunderstood for centuries and is now very rare; the fox has been hunted for its fur and despised for its wily ways; and the coyote is much hated, especially by sheep herders, who have tried unsuccessfully to eradicate the animal throughout its range. Nevertheless, there is much to admire in these relatives of Rover, for they are highly intelligent and social, unlike most other predatory animals, and they are not nearly as harmful to man as history would have us think.

The timber wolf, which is currently an endangered species because of man's invasion of its habitat and attempts to kill it to protect game and livestock, is now found mostly in

*The gray or timber wolf, although a fearsome beast by legend, is actually
an attractive social animal that pairs for life and is very shy of humans,
who have nevertheless tried to eradicate it over the years.*
(Tom McHugh)

The red fox is another successful member of the wild canine group, being shy, intelligent, and a good runner, whether on the prowl for rodents or on the run from hunters. (Leonard Lee Rue III; see page 70.)

Canada, though it once roamed most of the North American continent. Timber wolves cover a large territory, often of several hundred square miles, traveling in packs to follow their prey, usually deer, moose, and caribou, which are large enough to require a group-hunting effort. Although wolves can run as fast as thirty miles per hour, they do not usually try to run down their targets but prefer to use ambushing techniques or to trap animals in deep snow. Because of its smaller size, a wolf will not attack a full-grown moose, for instance, since it would have difficulty bringing the animal down and could be injured in the process. The average wolf pack numbers about half a dozen, often members of the same family, led by the dominant male. They communicate with each other vocally, howling intermittently to locate each other and to prepare for hunting. One female in the pack will give birth in the spring in a den to which other members of the pack will return after hunting, regurgitating food for the pups and their mother.

The coyote has many of the same characteristics as the wolf, although it is far more successful in its range, which is much of the United States (except for the Southeast) and southern and western Canada up into Alaska. (One reason for the coyote's increasingly wide range may be due to the diminished population of the wolf.) Like timber wolves, coyotes live in packs and will bark to communicate with one another. They do not hunt together unless they are trying to kill a large animal; most coyotes feed on rodents, snakes, frogs, and toads, as well as carrion and fruit. This ability to eat nearly anything may account for the coyote's success in spite of man's efforts to exterminate it as a pest or for its fur, which is increasingly valuable. The female coyote will have her pups in a den that she has dug herself or adapted from the burrow of another animal. The average litter is about half a dozen, but coyotes have been known to produce as many as eighteen young in one litter. The mother coyote is very protective and may employ the services of "aunts," other female coyotes without pups, to help raise her young, feeding them regurgitated meat and eventually teaching them to hunt for themselves.

The arctic fox is native to the northernmost parts of North America. It turns white in winter, good camouflage in the snow. (Joe Rychetnik; see page 70.)

Like the coyote, the red fox is fairly widespread and common, ranging through most of the United States (except for the Southwest) and Canada and Alaska. Once the animal ranged primarily in the North, but because of the importation of foxes from Europe for the sport of hunting, the species has expanded its range, much of it in competition with the coyote. Like the coyote, the various species of foxes feed on rodents, birds, and rabbits, but are even more omnivorous, preferring fruits and berries in summer as well as insects throughout the year. They are shy and solitary and are active primarily at night. The swift fox and the closely related kit fox are found in the Midwest and Southwest, while the gray fox is native to the East and Southwest. The gray fox is the only American member of the canid family that can climb and will occasionally hide and even forage for food in trees. Unlike the other foxes, it will use a den all winter, making a nest in a cave or hollow log where the female will raise her young in early spring. Although foxes do not live in packs, the male will usually help the female raise her young. The arctic fox, native to northern Canada and

Alaska, is well adapted to its extreme habitat; it has short legs and ears that are less apt to be frostbitten, fur-covered foot pads, and a thick coat that turns from brown or gray to white in the winter. In summer, the arctic fox will store food for winter and will sometimes rely on polar bears' leftovers. The fox preys mostly on rodents, preferring lemmings, whose population explosions every four years temporarily increase the fox population. Arctic foxes also eat berries, eggs, fish, and small rodents, and they may migrate south during the winter when food is scarce.

BEARS

Although many different animals live in the Arctic, the word *arctic* actually comes from the Greek word for "bear," suggesting that early explorers thought of the polar region as bear country. Although only the polar bear lives almost entirely in the Arctic, the other North American bears—the black and brown bears, including the grizzly—live primarily in Canada and Alaska; only the black bear exists in

The black bear, which in some parts of its range is brown, blue, or white, is more common in the United States than the other bears and was the model for the original Teddy bear, though it is hardly cuddly. (Helen Williams)

The grizzly bear, one of America's most impressive animals, will occasionally stand on two feet to take a look around or to threaten an intruder, but it usually travels on all fours and can, if pressed, run as fast as a horse. (Tom McHugh)

any numbers in the lower states. They were once more widespread but have been hunted out or have moved out of their original range. They are the largest land carnivores (the Kodiak bear can weigh nearly a ton) and though normally shy can be aggressive when provoked. They tend to be solitary except during breeding season or when food is plentiful; they gorge themselves in the autumn to survive the winter, at which time they den up to sleep, though they do not truly hibernate. Every other year, females give birth while still in the den to two or more cubs, which often weigh less than a pound—incredible given their eventual size!

The adult black bear may weigh as much as five hundred or six hundred pounds but is usually much smaller, two hundred pounds or less. Nevertheless, it is considerably larger than its namesake, the Teddy bear, which has become so popular throughout the world since Teddy Roosevelt befriended a black bear cub in 1902. Black bears are clumsy when walking but can run fast (up to thirty miles per hour), climb trees with agility, and swim very well. Fish is a favorite food, but the black bear lives primarily on vegetation, including twigs, nuts, leaves, fruit, and berries; it will also eat the inner layer of tree bark and many different insects, including bees, which it eats along with the honey. Like the other bears, black bears become dangerous when they lose their fear of man, as they do around dumps or parks where food is available.

The brown bear is a more formidable creature. There are several races of brown bear throughout the northern hemisphere. The grizzly is native to Canada and parts of the United States (though there are only a few hundred left in this country), and the closely related Kodiak or Alaskan brown bear ranges farther north and west. Considered by many the most unpredictable and dangerous of bears, the full-grown male Kodiak at sixteen hundred pounds or more is certainly the largest. The grizzly bear and its kin are omnivorous, like the black bear, feeding on plants, berries, fish, carrion, small rodents, and sometimes mammals. They

The polar bear is ideally equipped to live in an icy environment—camouflaged by its white color and kept warm by its large size, dense coat, and furry feet.
(Dan Guravich)

store food for occasional dining when they have killed more than they can eat, although in winter they live on stored body fat in their dens.

Brown bears are usually nocturnal and shy of man, but when they are surprised or protecting their young, they are capable of attacking in fury, rising up on their hind legs and using their teeth and front claws to bring down intruders. All brown bears have a prominent hump on their backs and a slightly concave face, giving them a distinctive appearance that most people both admire and fear.

The polar bear is quite different from the other North American bears, being pure white and equipped with fur-covered foot pads that give good traction and insulation on ice and snow. The hairs of its coat are hollow near the base, giving buoyancy in water as well as insulation. Polar bears are active during the day, and because vegetation is scarce in their habitat, they are far more carnivorous than the other bears, feeding on fish, seals, and walruses as well as shellfish and berries and mushrooms, when available. Polar bears may den up during the winter, though males are sometimes active even then; their dens are usually in the snow, although they will dig into the permafrost layer of earth in the southern part of their range, along Hudson Bay. Once hunted for fur and sport, polar bears are now protected and appear to be in no danger of extinction as was once thought; they are vulnerable to pollution, however, and since they have litters only every two or three years, their population could be severely affected if pollution is not quickly controlled.

THE CAT FAMILY

Although all of the carnivores we have met so far have been effective hunters, the cats are probably the most efficient hunters of all. Certainly they are beautifully designed for hunting, especially at night. All cats have excellent eyesight, with the ability to utilize all available light. Their hearing is superb, and they can use their sensitive whiskers

The jaguar is the only North American cat that roars, and it is also the largest of our wild cats, as well as the rarest, seen now mostly in South and Central America. (Tom McHugh, Wildlife Unlimited; see page 75.)

to gauge the distance between objects when they move. Their bodies are sleek and powerful, with sharp claws and strong jaws bearing long canine teeth. Although cats can run, climb, and even swim, they prefer to stalk their prey at close range and use ambush or the element of surprise rather than exhausting themselves chasing prey. The largest wild cat in North America is the jaguar, which weighs up to three hundred pounds. Though it travels great distances in search of food, it is rarely seen any longer north of Mexico. It feeds on peccaries and rodents, but will also take fish and sea-turtle eggs, since it likes water and will even play in pools on hot days. Other South and Central American cats once relatively common in the southern states but now scarce there are the ocelot, the margay, and

the jaguarundi. The first two are small spotted cats, which feed on small rodents, reptiles, and even birds, since they are excellent climbers and spend much time in trees. They have been severely reduced by the fur and pet trades as well as habitat destruction and are now protected by law in this country. The jaguarundi is not spotted but is also small. Little is known of its habits except that it can run very fast and can swim well, preying on fish as well as small rodents, poultry, and rabbits.

The mountain lion, which is also known as the cougar, puma, and catamount, is much larger, weighing up to two hundred pounds, and is still the most widely distributed carnivore in the western hemisphere. Because it requires a large territory for hunting, its present range is restricted by human habitation to the western states and occasionally the Southeast, as well as South and Central America. The mountain lion preys on deer, which it will follow for many miles, even outrunning them for short spurts. It prefers to

The mountain lion is a far more formidable predator than the other wild cats, being large and fairly widespread in the western part of North America.
(Tommy Lark, Western Ways)

The jaguarundi is another small cat of the Southwest, weighing less than twenty pounds and only rarely seen north of Mexico.
(G. C. Kelley)

The lynx, like its principal prey the snowshoe hare, has furred feet and long hind legs, giving it the ability to run quickly through the snow. (Tom Branch)

ambush its prey, however, and can leap more than twenty feet onto an animal's back, killing it instantly. When deer are not plentiful, the mountain lion will feed on smaller animals, including raccoons, porcupines and other rodents, coyotes, birds, livestock, and even insects. Mountain lions are hunted themselves by man, and where they are rare are protected by law. Although the adult mountain lion has a tawny color, the young cubs are spotted, presumably for protective purposes. The female lion will have one litter a year, and she raises it herself, since the male joins her only for a brief breeding period.

Unlike the mountain lion, the lynx is rarely a threat to man or livestock, preferring to prey on the snowshoe hare, rodents, birds, and carrion left by other, larger predators. The lynx lives in the deep forests of Canada and Alaska and is well adapted to the northern climates, with broad, fur-covered paws that enable it to walk on snow and long, thick fur much prized by furriers, who have helped make it rare in much of its original range—Europe, Asia, and much of the United States. The bobcat, although still rare, is more common in the southern half of North America, having adapted to life in the desert and high mountains. The bobcat is a smaller species of lynx, with the same short tail (hence its name) and high hind legs for pouncing, but less prominent ear tufts and shorter fur. The fur of both species is mottled, serving not so much as protection from predators as for camouflage in hunting. Although the bobcat preys mostly on hares, rabbits, and rodents, it will also feed on bats and even small livestock. Nevertheless, they are preyed upon themselves, mostly by man, who kills them as pests, for sport, or for their fur, which is increasingly valuable. Both the lynx and the bobcat are shy but can fight ferociously if cornered, and both are solitary, although the mother cats will keep their kittens with them for several months, teaching them to hunt and fend for themselves.

The bobcat, a southern member of the lynx family, lives in many parts of the United States, although it too is heavily hunted for its fur. (L. West)

MARINE MAMMALS

The harbor seal is a common sight on the shorelines of the northern regions of North America. They bask on the shore in groups but dive into the water at the first sign of danger. (Tom McHugh; see page 82.)

We have already met two mammals that have adapted well to life in and around the sea—the polar bear and the sea otter—as well as some other species that spend much time in fresh water—the muskrat and beaver. The animals in this chapter, however, are even more highly evolved in their seagoing existence, in both appearance and behavior. All but one of them are technically carnivores, feeding almost exclusively on meat, fish, or crustaceans, but most biologists place them in two different orders—the pinnipeds (or finned-feet animals), which include the seals, sea lions, and walruses; and the cetaceans, which include the whales, dolphins, and porpoises. Each of these mammals evolved ultimately from a land animal, and it is interesting to note

that each group we meet will become increasingly more fishlike, with flippers or fins instead of legs, with smooth fur or none at all, and with the ability to dive deep and remain underwater for long periods of time. Nevertheless, each of these species is not a fish but a mammal, breathing air as we do and suckling its young. Most of them are rather large, with thick layers of fat beneath the skin to serve as insulation in cold water, and all of them are superb swimmers, thanks to their streamlined bodies.

THE FIN-FOOTED SEALS

The eared seals as a group are found worldwide, but the most common species in North America are the fur seals and the California and northern sea lions. As their name suggests, they have distinctive external ears. Though their limbs are flippers well designed for swimming, they can also

The northern fur seal rarely comes on land, but when it does, it lives in breeding colonies or rookeries, where the biggest bulls form large harems of females. (George Holton; see page 80.)

get about on land, occasionally at impressive speeds. They spend most of their time at sea, often migrating many miles to follow fish and to avoid pack ice in the northern part of their range, but they congregate in large numbers during the breeding season in rookeries, where males, or bulls, will keep harems of cows with their young. The pups are born with fur and can swim within a few weeks, though they remain on land for several months and stay with their mothers for a year or more.

The northern fur seal, which ranges on the western coast to Alaska, has a thick undercoat, covered with a layer of guard hairs, that together with the blubber beneath protects the animal in the cold water. It migrates farther than the other eared seals, as far as six thousand miles, but generally breeds in the Bering Sea. The rookery on the Pribilof Islands is famous—not only for its size, which can be as great as a million seals, but also as an example of effective conservation. Once nearly wiped out by hunters, the fur seals there have been carefully managed by conservationists and have grown back to their original populations. The Guadalupe fur seal is much rarer, numbering perhaps a thousand animals and breeding only on Guadalupe Island off the coast of California; once reduced to a population of seven, the seal is now fully protected.

The Steller's or northern sea lion is much larger, the male weighing as much as a ton at ten feet long (fur seals are only about seven feet long). This animal is found on both sides of the Pacific and ranges in North America from California to the Aleutian Islands. It stays fairly close to land, feeding on fish but also on squid, clams, and other commercially important seafood. California sea lions are smaller and quite slender and are best known to humans as trained seals in circuses. They swim very fast—up to twenty-five miles per hour—and are very agile in the water, frolicking and playing as well as diving very deep to find

The harp seal, like many others in its family, bears a single offspring that is white at birth, well hidden against the snow-covered ice where it spends its first few weeks. As the seal matures, it will become darker in color and molt its coat each year, usually in April before migrating north for the summer.
(William R. Curtsinger; see page 82.)

fish. They remain on land during the day and generally fish at night, and are themselves preyed upon by killer whales and sharks. These sea lions are very vocal indeed, the males constantly barking and roaring to defend their harems and territories and the females conversing with their offspring, which recognize their mothers by their distinctive calls. Like fur seals, sea lions have been hunted in the past but are now protected by law.

The earless or hair seal group is very widespread and more exclusively aquatic than the eared seals. They do not have visible external ears—though their hearing is excellent—and their flippers are virtually useless on land. With a few exceptions, most North American seals in this group prefer the northern waters of Alaska, northern Canada, and the North Atlantic, staying beneath the ice and coming ashore or onto the ice to breed and raise their young. The young seals are usually born with a furry white coat that camouflages them on the ice and snow. The white coat is shed after a month and replaced by a darker adult coat better adapted to absorb heat. The harbor seal is easier to find than most, since it is common on both coasts and remains near shore, often basking on rocks and beaches in large groups. The ribbon seal, which has distinctive bands on its coat, is similar in size (up to two hundred pounds) but tends to stay away from shore and is relatively solitary, so it is much harder to spot. The harp seal, which has been the subject of much controversy because of the efforts of conservationists to prevent the hunting of the pure-white pups, is somewhat larger and migrates great distances, mostly in the North Atlantic, and it breeds on the ice off Newfoundland and Greenland. The pups are fed rich milk at first, gaining up to a hundred pounds in two weeks, but are then left on the ice by their parents and have to use their accumulated fat to sustain themselves as they learn to swim and fish. This fast is simply a preview of what they will undergo each year as adults, for the adults spend several weeks without eating during the breeding season.

The other species of earless seals are larger and remain in

The northern elephant seal is much larger than the other seals. Its milk is richest in fat of all mammals, which enables its pup to gain nearly three hundred pounds during its first month. (F. Gohier)

The manatee is a slow-moving animal that spends all of its time in the water grazing on aquatic plants. It is found off the coast of Florida and is well known as the original "mermaid." (Douglas Faulkner)

the arctic waters through the year, coming out on the ice to breed and molt their coats. Of these, the largest is the elephant seal, which can weigh up to four tons (females are smaller—only one ton). These huge seals are found on the California coast and are odd-looking animals indeed, with long snouts that the males can inflate during the breeding season and use to make calls that can be heard for miles. They breed and give birth on beaches, but spend the rest of the year at sea; they can remain underwater for as long as forty minutes, diving as deep as two hundred feet. Other seals are prey to killer whales, polar bears, and sharks as well as humans, but the full-grown elephant seal is well protected by its size and, now, by the law, since the whaling industry came close to eliminating the species nearly one hundred years ago.

The walrus is also a large animal, weighing up to three thousand pounds, and though it is thought to be an evolved type of earless seal, it is quite different from seals in several ways. For one thing, walruses are almost hairless, with the exception of bristles on the face, and for another, both sexes grow large tusks that they will use in pulling them-

selves out of the water onto ice. They are also gregarious throughout the year, living in large groups that are segregated by sex only at breeding time. They remain on land longer than most seals, although they are excellent swimmers and can dive to great depths in search of mollusks and crustaceans, which they eat after discarding the shells. They will also take seals. Their own predators include polar bears and killer whales, as well as man, who has found their meat, blubber, ivory, bones, and skin useful. They are now protected by law, although the Eskimos, who have traditionally hunted the walrus, are still allowed to do so.

THE MERMAID

Although the elephant seal and the walrus seem elephantlike in several ways, there is a group of marine mammals that is actually much closer to the elephant in biological terms. Unlike the other mammals in this chapter, the animals in this group are completely herbivorous, and like elephants they have great molars that wear down and are replaced periodically. They also have thick hairless skin

Walruses often live in herds of a thousand or more, but they do not form harems. The bulls, however, do fight for dominance with their impressive tusks, which are also useful for protection against predators and for pulling themselves onto the ice.
(Carleton Ray; see page 83.)

with bristles around the muzzle, are very large, weighing up to a ton, and are native to tropical and subtropical areas, preferring warm weather to cold. Unlike elephants, however, these curious creatures are completely adapted to life underwater, and one of the species in the order, known as the manatee, is native to North America, inhabiting the waters off the coast of Florida. Christopher Columbus was possibly the first European ever to see manatees, and for many years they were believed by sailors to be mermaids, probably because of their habit of cradling their offspring at their breasts. Otherwise they are not particularly pretty animals, being very bulky, with flippers for forelegs and no hind legs at all. They do not swim rapidly as whales and seals do but tend to hang in the water or lie on the bottom, rising every few minutes to the surface to breathe. They graze constantly on aquatic vegetation, usually at night, and because they are not particularly alert, they are often injured by motorboat propellers. They are also sensitive to the presence of humans, who once hunted them for food, and are for that reason an endangered species, now protected by law.

The blue whale is the largest animal in the world, weighing up to 300,000 pounds, yet it feeds on tiny crustaceans no more than a few ounces in weight. (Russ Kinne)

WHALES AND DOLPHINS

Although these mammals still require air for breathing, they never leave the water, and their bodies are the most streamlined of all, with no hair, small flippers with no hind legs, rudderlike flukes or tails, and blowholes on the top of the head for breathing. There are two groups of whales: whalebone or baleen whales, which include some of the largest animals in the world; and toothed whales, which include the dolphins. All whales, like bats and some seals, use echolocation for direction, since their sense of hearing is better than their sense of sight. They make a series of sounds that bounce off objects and help them determine the presence of prey, and they also use a variety of sounds to maintain contact with each other. There are a number of whales that come into the waters around North America, but we shall single out three species only, because they are both spectacular and characteristic examples of this very special mammal.

The blue whale is not only the largest mammal in existence, it is undoubtedly the largest animal that has ever lived at any time, weighing up to 150 tons and measuring a hundred feet long. It is likely that the blue whale has never been very numerous, because of its size, but it is definitely rare now, because of its widespread destruction by the whaling industry. Although the Marine Mammal Act of 1972 protects it, along with most other whales, from being hunted, there are still a few countries that continue to kill this magnificent creature for oil, meat, and baleen, which was once used to make women's corsets. Baleen is actually a set of bony plates that hang down on either side inside the whale's mouth, which is exceptionally large. The feeding whale swims through the water, and the baleen strains out plankton or krill (a tiny shrimplike animal) as the water is forced out of the mouth, and these substances are the whale's principal sustenance. Blue whales are solitary, but most of the other baleen whales are not, swimming in large schools from the Arctic or Antarctic during the summer when the water is rich in food to the warmer waters during the winter, when they breed and give birth—all in the water, of course.

Most toothed whales, because they have teeth, can feed

The beluga whale is found in arctic waters, as one might guess from its white coloration; the baby whales are born gray and gradually lighten in color as they mature.
(J. R. Simon)

on fish and do not have to travel toward the poles in search of plankton, and they prefer the warmer waters of the tropical and temperate zones. The beluga or white whale does move into the Arctic—presumably the reason for its white coloration. It is smaller than the baleen whales (up to seventeen feet long) and often falls prey to the killer whale. The killer whale is not a true whale but a large dolphin, up to twenty-five feet long. It is found throughout the world, although it too likes the cold water of the North Atlantic and Pacific. It is a spectacularly marked black-and-white animal, and true to its name is an aggressive killer, going after seals and other whales as well as fish.

Unlike whales, dolphins have beaklike noses and are noted for their great leaps in the water, as they "porpoise" at high speed, often accompanying boats. (Oddly enough, porpoises, which are smaller than dolphins but otherwise quite similar, do not leap from the water.) There are many species in this family, but the best-known are the common dolphin, the bottlenose dolphin of the Atlantic, and the Pacific white-sided dolphin; the last two are often used as attractions at marine aquariums. Although man has hunted dolphins and porpoises in the past for meat, they are not hunted for themselves now but caught inadvertently in the nets of commercial fishermen. Most humans are interested in these animals because of their amazing intelligence, which has become obvious through various efforts to train them and keep them in captivity. We do not know as yet just how smart dolphins may be, but it is clear that they are certainly among the most intelligent beings on the planet with us. Given their general good nature and their friendly curiosity about us, it would be wonderful indeed to find out someday that they are as intelligent as humans, having evolved through the ages along a parallel but much different path, living in water and behaving peacefully, rather than trying to destroy their own habitat and that of the other animals that share the earth with them.

The bottlenose dolphin is one of the best swimmers—and perhaps also one of the most intelligent animals—in the world. (Russ Kinne)

SUGGESTED READING

There are many excellent books about the mammals of North America, some of them fairly scientific and others intended for the general reader. The best field guide available is *The Audubon Society Field Guide to North American Mammals*, written by John O. Whitaker, Jr., and published by Alfred A. Knopf. In addition to descriptions of each mammal, there are full-color photographs, range maps, and illustrations that show track marks, silhouettes, and other aids for the amateur naturalist. If you are interested in looking at North American mammals in relation to their rela-

tives throughout the world, *World Guide to Mammals* by Nicole Duplaix and Noel Simon, published by Greenwich House (distributed by Crown Publishers, Inc.), offers an excellent survey with full-color illustrations. There are also a number of books devoted to individual species or to groups of mammals, such as the whales and dolphins, and fascinating discussions of aspects of mammalian life, such as migration and evolution. These can be found in your bookstore or library.

INDEX OF MAMMALS